About the

Mary was born in Australia, lived in Malta and finally moved to the UK twenty years ago, where she currently lives.

She has kept a journal of her thoughts and life experiences since the age of sixteen. Her other publication so far, *Liberation at Long Last,* by M. Mallia (XLibris 2014), is a touching semi-autobiographical account, in novel form, of her inner journey alongside that of her mother's, inspired by her late mother's brutal suicide twenty years earlier. It depicts how despair and death are triumphantly overcome by love, faith and forgiveness.

Mary's love of poetry can be traced back to her secondary school days, but she only started writing poetry herself in the last three years.

A RETURN TO LOVE
TO THE HEART OF GOD

MARY M.

A RETURN TO LOVE
TO THE HEART OF GOD

Vanguard Press

VANGUARD PAPERBACK

© Copyright 2021
Mary M.

The right of Mary M. to be identified as author of
this work has been asserted by her in accordance with the
Copyright, Designs and Patents Act 1988.

All Rights Reserved

No reproduction, copy or transmission of this publication
may be made without written permission.
No paragraph of this publication may be reproduced,
copied or transmitted save with the written permission of the
publisher, or in accordance with the provisions
of the Copyright Act 1956 (as amended).

Any person who commits any unauthorised act in relation to
this publication may be liable to criminal
prosecution and civil claims for damages.

A CIP catalogue record for this title is
available from the British Library.

ISBN 978 1 784160 00 2

*Vanguard Press is an imprint of
Pegasus Elliot MacKenzie Publishers Ltd.*
www.pegasuspublishers.com

First Published in 2021

**Vanguard Press
Sheraton House Castle Park
Cambridge England**
Printed & Bound in Great Britain

Dedication

To Lord Jesus the Christ Consciousness, Son of the Heavenly Father — Divine Earthly Mother, breathed into the Virgin Mary by the Love, Life and Light of eternal Cosmic Consciousness or Holy Spirit all reverberating within eternal Divine Cosmic Sound.

Acknowledgements

I would like to thank my mother, Josephine, and her mother, Antonia, who are no longer with us, for the love they have given me throughout my whole life, whether they were there physically or in spirit. Their continued presence and support is always greatly appreciated. Thank you both so much.

I would also like to thank my two wonderful sons, Matthew and Daniel, each of whom has supported me in their own unique way throughout the putting together of this book. I have had to leave home — literally and metaphorically — quite a few times to get the experience and the inspiration needed to pen these verses, but both always welcomed me back with open arms and warm, loving, hearts.

Furthermore, I am very grateful for my friends, Patricia, Josephine, Alice, Doris and Helen, for their life-long friendship transcending time and space, and their unwavering belief in me as a friend and as a writer. Heartfelt thanks also go to my friends, Aileen, Anna, Ilona and Lindzi, who have stood by me as we traverse the tricky terrain of this earthly life, always trusting the process and our solid friendship.

Finally, I cannot but help be grateful to the Cosmic and Christ Consciousness which flows in and through me to create such a diverse collection of poems. My deep gratitude goes to all beings of love, life and light who in and from God have expressed in and through me this message of hope to a world in the depths of despair. A special mention also goes to Archangel Michael (aka Lord Mikaal) and the Divine Earthly Mother, Queen Aurora, for their beautiful contribution which makes the collection complete.

I am grateful that I have been found to be a worthy vehicle through which this message has been delivered to the world.

Contents

VOLUME I 15

   Heeding the Call — the Call of Love......... 17

   The Call of Love 18

   The First Step 20

   Heeding the Call.. 22

   Just Sitting.. 24

   Stripped Stark Naked 26

   The Test.. 30

   The Struggle... 33

   The Voice of Love Speaks.......................... 36

   The Transformation.................................... 39

   Dancing For Joy 43

   When She Calls, She Calls......................... 45

   The Meeting 47

VOLUME II 51

   Return to LOVE — A Return to the Heart of GOD 53

   A Return to Love 54

   Here I Come 56

   The Mother's Yes 60

The Journey Must Go On 62

Love 67

Light 69

Life 75

The Presence 79

Surrendering 81

Love's Reassuring Words 83

The Calming of the Storm 85

The Sound Summons 89

VOLUME III 91

Mother and Son Reunited their Love
Reignited I 93

Mother and Son Reunited and their Love
Reignited II 94

Michael Mother and Son 101

The Birth 105

The Mother goes to Bethlehem (on the Feast
of the Immaculate Conception) 107

Mother, Son and Everyone 111

The Two Mothers 113

The Son to His Mother I 116

The Son To His Mother II 117

The Son to His Mother III 120

The Heavenly Father to the Virgin Mother
.... 123

Mother and Son — 125

A Dialogue 125

Mother to Son.. 129

VOLUME IV 131

Back Home, Where We Belong! 133

The One in All, the All in One 134

A New Heaven, A New Earth.................... 137

Hallelujah 140

Oh, Blessed Day...................................... 142

Leaping Legs, Skipping Feet.................... 144

God Speaks Through the Mist in Avalon . 146

Light Over Darkness Wins 149

The Virgin's Prayer 151

(For the Divine Earthly Mother) 151

I Am Enough 154

Going Forth 156

The |Love of the Father, Mother and Son 158

The Whisper of Your Inner Voice............. 160

EPILOGUE 165

The Red Admiral 1657

VOLUME I

Heeding the Call — the Call of Love

This the time to go within,
In a deep silence free from the din.
Opening the door of your heart, its music comes
And of Love, peace and joy it sweetly hums.
As you sit calmly and quietly still
allowing its Love within — your whole Being to fill.
And when the door opens, this Love like a sunbeam
will illuminate your world — your whole, entire Being.
The heavy load lightens,
darkness it frightens,
loud noises soften
as ears slowly open.
How it rejoices with each heart that anew
opens the door, letting the Light shine through.
This aspect of the Godhead we sometimes forget,
as its Law of Love we don't always get.

The Call of Love

Heed the call of Love that summons from the Eternal
Space within
Listen intently to its calling as its beating heart sings
therein
Of Love's Infinite Life, Peace and Joy as they dance
To its beating rhythm within and without, as in a
trance.

Dancing joyfully, celebrating Love's lust for Life,
Letting go of all fear, anger and strife.
Allowing it to flow forth freely and trusting it will
Flood your whole Being and beyond with its peace, so
tranquil.

Do not doubt for a minute that this is not so
Trust fully in your Souls own ability to glow
In your own Soul's bliss and joy as it brings forth
Your own inner spirit from west, south, east and north.

Gathering its bits scattered across the Earth and outer
space,
Scraps that had been lost and fallen from grace
suddenly reappear to be made whole
graciously united Mind, Body, Heart and Soul,
into one complete being as was always intended

from the beginning of time your Soul's purpose depended
On Love flowing forth with no hindrance or blockage suspended,
Love's true path cleared and resplendent
with beautiful jewels and a garment of silk
with a golden treasure trove of bright light, whose ilk
Is to fill your whole Being and that of the Earth
Heavens, waters, trees, flowers and hearth

With a wholeness whose Peace and Love forever abide
With a wholeness whose Peace and Life never subside
With a wholeness whose Joy wipes away all our tears
With a wholeness whose Light chases away all our fears.

And so, perhaps just for today take a moment of stillness and rest
As I graciously invite you this theory to test.
Listening intently to Love's own song and calling
Wait in the shade underneath its cool awning
As it sings to you of your own Divine stature
As it dances its dance of a Spiritual nature
Your heart will flutter and your body rejoice
As Love's calling whispers of Unity
Harmony
Joy.

The First Step

Walking ahead with our heads held up high
Our true own Being, we embrace not deny.
Our Beings alive, accepted and beheld
Our power is claimed, nothing is withheld.

Our very own true power to be loved and to love
Without any fear, but as free as a dove.
Our own true desire for a connection that's true,
Comes from deep within me and deep within you.

We seek outside what lies so latent within
We look outside for what lies hidden, therein
When we pause still for a moment or two
It comes rushing at us with glee, at me and at you.

It wants to burst forth, this Power trapped in a small confine
It wants to be free to fly, space to redefine.
To soar to new places, new views, new sights
To sample Life's simple, yet delicious delights!

It doesn't want to stay caged, trapped anymore
Its spirit is strong and away wants to soar.
To realise its power to glide and to roam
Acknowledging Who and What it is, it can fly freely
back home.

Home is not a confined, dark, angry cage
stone-cold, fearful, full of rage.
Home is filled with Life, Light and Delight -
Home is where the Soul rests after its flight!

Heeding the Call

Heeding the Call of the Dawn of Being
Welcoming the day of when by your own seeing,
Your heart opens gently at the sides,
The door to where pure Love abides.

The door is ajar, opening fully soon,
overlooking a garden with a bright silver moon.
The key is ever so slowly turning
Love's Desire to Love — its yearning!

The heart desires to love and to be loved
The aspects of Lover, Loved, Beloved,
From the Beginning of Time Immortal
Journeys to the Soul's own Loving portal.

And through the motions of life's ups and downs
through our everyday smiles and occasional frowns
above and beyond all our hopes and freezing Fears
Love's compassionate blanket dries away all our tears.

There is no division, rejection or untrue words and
deeds —
True Love the Soul of Lover and Beloved feeds.
"Is this humanly possible?" some may ask,
"All day and night in the warmth of true Love to bask?"

Within each and every one of us mere human
embodiment
Lives a Force within so pure, so peaceful, so content
Not realised for What or Who it truly is and What it can
do,
Its underestimated Truth and Power too.

Lying dormant, asleep, awakening from deep slumber
with caring compassion and joy, our hearts beckoning.
Overflowing, it fills the whole of our Being and
everywhere
Our True Being realised, Love springs forth abundantly,
with ever more to spare.

Just Sitting

When life's troubles come and spin you right round
Let the weary body rest in Spirit's own sound.
The sound of the Universe speaking to you,
Just listen intently, not much more you can do!

As we graciously sit and within our own Being
we gently look with our own inner seeing —
We judge not the whys and wherefores
We only sit allowing it all to slowly surface.
We simply sit, allowing it all to be there
free from judging, free from fear of just being laid
bare.
As We silently sit and gently stare
out into the space ahead with eyes softly open, we rest
our gaze
into the space in front, inside and beyond
on the Spaciousness of Space and the Fearlessness of
Pure Being.

In the midst of thoughts, actions, naming and shaming
We are not our thoughts, we are not our mind's gaming
We are not our words, our deeds, actions or thinking,
We are not the dark patches that cause all our blinking.

On careful examination, after just sitting with spacious
gaze
the comings and goings of the busy mind and its
confusing haze
You come to a point of Knowing deep inside
The warm golden glow and bright silvery white Light
that in our hearts abide.
Without further ado and with courage and resolve
let's allow this warm bright white healing Light in our
hearts to dissolve
in the depths of our Being, inside deep within
where nothing can change it… diminish it… or
deplete it… allowing it to rest, therein.

Stripped Stark Naked

"But how do we cope when we feel like life has
stripped us naked and we cannot dance but want to
hide, when we cannot leap for joy as we are dying
inside?"

Stripped naked with nothing left inside
Stark naked with nowhere left to hide.
No shiny silk adorned garments and golden crowns for
me
Just a plain ache… a pain… a hurt… nothing pleasant
to see.

Stark naked crawling on the dirty, dusty floor
Stark naked my shining light seems light no more.
Darkness covers my legs, my belly, my chest, my face,
my head
There is no light, but fear and anger filling my body
instead.

I slowly fumble along the dark-filled room
stagger slowly as the dim light is fading soon.

A dark cloud envelops my whole body and spirit
I strain my eyes, my ears and am tested to the limit.

Wherever I turn there is a void and an emptiness
Wherever I turn I try to see happiness -
But, like a butterfly fluttering it quickly eludes me
Leaving my heart, body and bones stripped of glee.

Where do I go from here, what do I do?
I can't at the mo' be happy like you, you or you!
My heart shudders, my body trembles and shakes
A sadness, a fear, an anger, my peace from my Being
takes!

Just for now take a deep breath and rest
Just for now be still — this too will pass, this test!
Just for this moment, glance at the sky
Relish this breath, as you take a deep sigh!

Look in the mirror and gaze lovingly at what you see
A beautiful person looking back at you and me.
Made in the image and liking of the Godhead Divine
our bodies, do not our Being define and confine!

So, look a bit more closely with a kind, loving open heart
there, in the chest in the mirror a warm glow is about to start
Allow it to spread... e-x-p-a-n-d... fill your whole body,
from toe right up to the head to embody.

The warm golden glow in the mirror comes closer to me.
The bright silvery light in the mirror is what I can clearly see.
Filling and settling into my own heart, mind, body and chest,
bringing my whole Being momentarily to a place of unity, to rest!

I stand (or sit) there with feet wide apart
I stand (or sit) there with the warming glow still in my heart
I stand (or sit) there breathing softly in and out...
I stand (or sit) there as the gentle glow spreads slowly about.

It continues to expand throughout the whole of my
Being
filling now all my cells with its Love, as my eyes
seeing
not the physical body, but the Divine glow within me
My true Divine nature I now freely embrace and
embody.

The Test

When it's like the beaten track is wearing you down
and all you want to do is up and leave town
just take a minute to breathe, rest and repose,
until the time comes for the test to pass — I suppose!

The test is not always a simple task.
Sometimes it seems you have to wear a mask
of smiling, chirping, dancing and thinking
when deep down inside your heart is sinking.

It is at times like this that this bright, white healing
Light
as purified gold, luminous silver Life and Love abide
It longs your entire whole being to fill
so, pause for a moment and be quiet, be still.

So that resting in its warm and soft embrace
your whole being begins to feel full of Grace.
This Love unconditional, so pure and so Divine
our whole world view, springs forth to redefine.

It sustains our whole existence today and always
It protects us through life's dark mysterious alleyways
It lights up many a deserted street

in which no kindred soul you are likely to meet.

And yet, as you rest in the comfort of its warm gentle
glow
a Light shines through each and every row
of houses, in the here and now as we walk
with our warm golden glow within we talk
 Of loves lost and of loves that have been found
of labels, names and games that the mind do confound
of dark, dreary days when we seem to forget
the warm Golden Glow within is already there, set!

To comfort us with its warmth and luminous Light
to make us whole again as it shines so bright
reminding us of the Love that lays inside
ready to forge forth with Power and Might.

With Kindness, Compassion, Patience and Wisdom
Love within us establishes its luminous, live Kingdom
Putting all the wrongs right and setting us straight
our past… our futures… and our present, as we
patiently wait

For its Bright Silver Ray, Warm Golden Glow to beam
filling the whole Body and Mind to the brim, and
beyond it does seem

to settle through our Beings and fill the Soul with
contentment
Our whole Being and beyond in its gentle warm glow,
to cement.

And when this union so pure, so Divine
this place within in which everything's fine.
There is no past or future to see,
There our Souls rest, there, inside you and me.

The Struggle

It is pure Love
With no limits or boundaries
filling whole nations and entire countries.

The only challenge is our defence
built to keep it out, our offence
As we mock its Divine Love and plan:

"Come in, only if you can!"

"I cannot come in if you block Me out.
Your defences are up as I hear you shout." (God replies)

"I'm so scared to let You in,
amidst my chaos and my din.
I'm ashamed of my state of affairs,
anyway, in my life nobody cares.
I walk ahead alone, abandoned, dejected,
The Laws of Love I have rejected.
There's nobody out there for me,
I walk all alone as you can see.
I take pride in stumbling, weak upon the ground

and await constantly for when the next fall will come
around.
It doesn't occur to me there may be another way,
although I have heard and have known others say
that the Christ's been born, a new way to teach
so that humankind Harmony and Peace do reach.
I can see, my ways have been terribly skewed,
My Being is trampled and it needs renewed.

Alas, as I fall
for help I do call
but nobody's around
and they can't hear the sound
of my silent anguish and pain.
Writhing inside, in agony again and again,
determined from this dejected life to refrain.
Shedding tears of acid rain
in this state I can't remain.
What to do? Where to go?
I'm waking up, please let me know."

"Go the the centre of your heart, there (replies God)
in fullness and sweetness is where
My Love lives within you and My Life too,

stop what you're doing and put on your shoe!
Let's undertake the longest journey so far,
the one from your busy head to your illumed heart
where there is no past or fearfully, frightening future to
dread,
just the warmth of Love on the path that you silently
tread."

The Voice of Love Speaks

In front of the mirror you sit or stand tall
In front of the mirror you feel great, big, little or small.
Close your eyes softly, momentarily for the mirror to
see
It is not out there on the wall, but inside you and me.

Tread gently and carefully, go softly and with care
for a thumping pace the still Presence inside is likely to
scare -
and in the chest part of the body where the heart lies
inside
the warm soft silvery light and golden glow silently
abide.

Amidst all the labels, the names and the games
Amongst all the judging, the fears and the shames,
Silently hidden in the deep recesses of every heart
Is a silent deep Peace, Wisdom and Light all enveloped
in Love.

The Love within whispers quietly: "Do not be afraid
come in a bit closer, it's OK, it's OK.
I've been waiting ardently for the day you would
come,

I'm ever so joyfully and compassionately present, my
welcome's just begun!

I welcome you profusely to the Source of your very
own Being
The place accessible only through your eyes' inner
seeing.
I do not judge through names, labels, guilt, anger or
fear
You're welcome through the unconditional Love that is
here
Never a word or thought of judgement or shame
Never daring or wanting to point a finger and blame.

 I have sat and waited, longing for you to come home
to Me
Your awareness resting in this place deep within, full
of glee.
I ask no questions like why, what, where or how?
I just take you as you are in the Here, in the Now."

And just as we have simply been lying down, sitting or
standing,
Gently let go of all the unnecessary din, understanding
That this warm bright healing white Light that lies
therein

Is, has and forever will be eagerly, silently waiting
within.

For the few moments each day to which towards it we
draw
our busy attention which is busy no more,
For quietly we rest in the warmth, peace and stillness
our body's respose, our soul's yearning, our own
mind's willingness.

The Transformation

When the pains that come up, that ache deep inside
when feelings of dread greeting each morning abide,
When the fear of the future so pertinent and seemingly
true
the fear of something void of its own being, untrue.

A freezing fear that can weaken body and spirit
A daunting dread that our life chances limit —
A fear so grotesque, so monstrous, so perverse
It seems to cripple our whole Universe.

For the heart it shuts to Love and to trust
A veil of mistrust over the heart gathers dust
As it numbs the hearts rhythm, silences its beats
Making all successes seem more like defeats.

In the ensuing confusion, anger and crippling fear
the bright silvery light, golden glow doesn't seem at all
near,
covered so aptly with a dusty silk veil
perhaps kept in place with a rusty old nail!

The bright silvery light and warm golden glow inside
want to shine outwards from where they reside

filling your whole Being within and the universe too
with Its warmth, peace and joy as they otherwise
would do.

Suddenly the veil moves and the dust gently rises
the whole of the body and mind confused by surprises,
are shocked to the core of this movement, they shudder
they don't want any more movement, and yet
another…
Shift gently and slowly makes the veil move ever so
slightly
the veil and the dust move ever so lightly,
sliding softly to the side, further to the side
allowing the light to shine through a gap created
inside.

Through the gap in the veil the pure silvery light and
golden glow
Shine right through ever so bright and do flow
Lighting up the whole of the chest, the back and
beyond
the dust disappears in the commotion in a split of a
second.
The veil's allowed to slip through the hole
The veil slides and slithers away from the soul,
Unblocking the light, uncovering the glow

Freedom at last from the dust and the veil. So,

Unexpectedly, and yet so joyfully and graciously greeted
seemingly mind, body and soul are united and seated
Once more at the throne deep within one's own being secured
The bright silvery light, warm golden glow their presence procured.

In the presence of the bright silvery ray of Life and Love
there is a white purity like the innocence of a dove
there is peace, joy and a still serenity.
Rest there for a while, so that you can see

And experience with your own Awareness and Mind
that within the body and the mind does abide
a shimmering Presence golden, silver and white so sublime,
rest your gaze, have a look, an experience Divine!

Of what lies beyond the names, the labels and the fears
of what lies beyond conditioning, brain washing and tears
of what cannot properly by words be described

can only be experienced through an open and willing
Heart and Mind.

Allow the Heart, Mind, Awareness and Consciousness
to rest
Open, trusting and spacious this theory to test
do not take what I say as being totally true,
experience it directly for you... yes, for you!

Dancing For Joy

In a quiet shady corner, I hope you took some time to rest
Your weary soul and battered body may have seemed
rested in a luminous glow gleamed.

Allowing the eyes… the ears… the jaw and the body to soften
a sense of spaciousness a sense of light can very often
begin to pervade our Consciousness… our Heart…
our Mind… and Spirit
filling us through and through with pure Light without any limit.

The radiance of rays silvery soft with the glow of gold,
in the heart centre in the chest, Its abode,
with compassion and in a tender, loving embrace
touching the heart with Its Love and tender Grace.

Of Grace and Forgiveness, an Innocence too,
the heart is forgiven — Love's job is to undo
all the damaging damage that has ever been done
to set the heart free, for it NOW to have fun!

And enjoy this embodied Spirit being set free

radiating that pure golden gleam that's there inside me
not a beauty that fades, not a body that dies,
but a Soul full of Love defying space and time as it
flies
out to the Universe, as free as a bird
silently soaring not uttering a word
filling your Body, your Heart, your Soul and your
Mind
with a gentle loving peace and joy you will find.

I humbly invite you to engage with some of these
practices
as Heart, Mind, Body and Spirit come together I'm
saying
Dancing swiftly, swirling and gleefully playing
down your Soul's own path without any further
delaying.
As the Godhead in the distance your footsteps can hear
They approach very softly coming quietly nearer and
nearer.
The exquisite Divine Dance of your journey's begun,
Now let's all join in within and just have some fun!

When She Calls, She Calls

Today as I walked I heard the sound of the Land,
through mud and rocks and shale and sand.
I looked around as the musical sound
Its way to my eager ears found.

She beckoned me to closer get
and to never what lies in my heart forget.
She urged me to climb up further along
from which spot, I heard this song:

"Come to me, darling, come to me, sweet,
loosen your tongue and quicken your feet.
I've awaited your coming for so long,
Come to me, darling, and join in my song."

Up the hill I hastened quickening my pace
A sense of urgency, pushed me up in haste.
I clambered and climbed to the very top
I'd climbed up far enough, I could now stop.

There on the summit on the top of the tor,
A voice came a-calling from the sweet portal's door.
I listened intently as the wind whistled so
And the song, it continued, it continued to go:

"Come to me, darling, come to me, sweet,
loosen your tongue and quicken your feet.
I've awaited your coming, Oh for so long,
Come to me, darling, and join in my song."

On the top of the tor, on the side somewhat steep
Her song gently whispered for my free feet to leap
And to boldly go through that sweet portal door
to go through trusting, in Faith — I shan't fall.

The portal it opened and lo and behold!
Visions of beauty exquisite like the days of old
When as a young maiden, angels did me visit
and in Heavenly voices sang songs so exquisite:

"Come to me, darling, come to me, sweet,
loosen your tongue and quicken your feet.
We've all awaited your coming, Oh for so long,
Come in, our dearest, and forevermore join in Our
song."

The Meeting

'The Meeting' takes place underneath an awning. I invite you to allow yourself to be transported to the most exquisite, beautiful and peaceful place where the awning or canopy might be, allowing your imagination to rest there, amidst the waterfalls, lush vegetation or sunsets and sunrises on beaches or hills. The sky's the limit and the Mind's got the skills to take you wherever you want to be!

Dearly Beloved Body you have heeded My call
Dearly Beloved Heart you are weary no more.
Dearly Beloved Spirit you have been set free
Dearly Beloved Mind you can now so clearly see

The indisputable Essence of Who and What You truly are
beyond all the labels, names and shames, albeit quite bizarre,
lies a Love full of Life and a Joy so sublime
a gracious Compassion, a Forgiveness Divine.

As in this Absolute Truth of Love you rest
the Truth of your Being is now at its best
with no past or future to worry about and fret,

just resting in Love, is true resting, I bet!

And as you lounge in the sunshine of Love's true
abode
and nonchalantly wander up and down its true road
an exciting adventure is about to begin, as you meet
like-minded Hearts and Souls up and down every
street.

They too, like you have heard My Love calling
They too, like you have rested in the shade of Its
awning
They too like you have danced to its rhythm and beat
They too like you wander with a heartbeat in the soles
of their feet!

As you walk ahead, you are pleasantly surprised and
glad
that you too have opened your ears and clearly heard
the soothing lullaby of Love's gently whispered song
and that you too are now joyfully singing along!

We are all so pleasantly surprised and in awe when
the joys of Love unite us, We are all One then
there is no you and I, no me and you
there is only Love with nothing to do.

But, to rest in My awning all gathered as One.
Just rest in the shade as your journey's begun.
The warmth from the sun makes the heart shine so
bright
the Love within shines outwards, such a luminous
Light.

All the others under the awning with you can feel
the soft warm love within as it glows so genteel
filling each and every One with its white silvery light
and golden beam
filling each one with a Life, and Light Supreme!

VOLUME II

Return to LOVE — A Return to the Heart of GOD

And the sweet Mother goes,
caution to the wind, she throws
back to God's Loving Heart
of which YOU (Dear Reader) are also a part
on this journey you're invited to join her
As she'll gently guide you on your way there.

"Ahead I go forth, trust I must
That God's plan, albeit hard will unfold and work out
for my highest good and the highest good of all
Humanity and all sentient beings.
Leaving the old, embracing the new
Heart, Mind, Body and Soul to renew.
Finding myself as I journey on,
My strengths, my fortes and things to learn from.
Forging new friendships, establishing new ties,
embracing the new as the old, unwanted dies.
Using my wings to soar above the stars
Courage, Confidence, Kindness fill my jars
with oil to light the lamp of my Soul,
keeping it topped up and lit, is my goal
with kindness, compassion and peace
as fear, guilt and shame I release."

A Return to Love

I am and have been restored.
In Body, Mind and Spirit
As Love me comes to visit.
Refilling my being with Its radiant Grace
Shining throughout my body, my face.
Reminding me of who I really am,
Divine.

A new Earth's coming, the birth's begun.
The head is crowning, the legs spread wide
Fear and fear of Death, are now put aside.
A new Life enters a New Heaven and Earth
And all creation will welcome it's birth.
The pure of heart, humbly come in
Free from fear, anger, guilt, shame or sin.
The clothes they wear as white as snow,
By pure Love enveloped, for this they know,
A Love so deep and all-embracing,
A Love that seeps deep into each fibre interlacing
And bringing forth wholeness, healing, peace and joy
A oneness, a unity, a harmony for each to enjoy.
The New Earth is Now and Here
Be love, peace, joy, denounce fear.
Allow your whole being to be embraced

With Life's beauty and sweetness to be always graced.
Allow your whole being to be restored
in the realms of Heaven to be adored.
To be welcomed back with a great feast, a celebration,
a party
dancing to the music,
moving to its beat
eating delicious morsels sweet.
Spinning around,
to the sound,
of Love freely pouring,
as your Spirit's soaring
up to the stars,
way beyond Mars.
To be one with
Now and forevermore.
So be it. Amen.

Here I Come

My ministry's begun,
Please, please follow my Son.
The Son of God the Most High
don't let this invite pass you by.
Instead, pause and sit or stand still
Until of His Love you'd had your fill.

Allow your whole Being to Him to belong
Your heart and your mind to sing His song
of joy and of gladness
of a Love like a madness
knowing no limits, no boundaries
no borders, no counties or countries.

But, that most precious human Soul
To touch it with His Presence, His goal.
It wakes up what is sleeping inside
bringing it slowly back to life.
Awakened inside your Being and beyond,
Your heart will dance to a brand-new song.

Allow Him in

to free you from sin
So that free inside
In Him you'll abide.
Making you One —
your soul and The Son.
He knows your heart
like a weather chart.
Your ups and downs,
Your smiles and frowns.
Your weaknesses and strengths
And will go to great lengths
to stabilise your climate.
A drizzle descends and comes down
refreshing your head and its crown.
That sin, like a scarlet red
turns to a pure white snow, instead.
Forgiving all that had taken place
restoring all with His gracious grace.
His Presence only in the here, in this moment,
His nature compassionate, kind, forgiving, clement.
His Love abundant, constant and everlasting
Beyond concepts can convey
or any words can ever say.

A love so pure, so intense, so deep
into the depths of your being It'll seep.
Changing your inner structure and restoring
the innermost of your being with sweetness adorning,
making you whole, not broken any more.
Here it is, to heal and restore.

Whenever plagued by doubt and fear
His presence within all that will clear.
As clear as day, as we sometimes say
keeping Fear and Doubt at bay.

So, put your trust in Him
in that pure Love which lies within
It will strengthen all therein.
It will set you free
Able to be
Loved and empowered, try it, you'll see.

Take all of this ever so lightly
And test it ever so blithely,
these practises that I put forward
and propose.
Be ever so ready

Quick and quite steady,
to make this journey your own.

The Truth sets you free,
but only you yourself can know,
through direct personal experience
The Truth.

The Mother's Yes

I shall go ahead,
With Nada in my head
Forging the way
Come what may
To do Your Will.

In me instil
Your Holy Grace
At a rapid pace (please!),
Acknowledge me
And let Your Divine Love fulfil me.
Give me courage to be
And eyes to see
Your Mary who
Goes out forth doing what she needs to do!

I realise now the power of evil
The destructive strength of the d*v*l.
Yet, I know you are more strong,
With You in me I can't go wrong.
Fully protected, Your Nada sound
Its full power, I've just found.
Although within me since the age of six or even before

I now know its value and power much more.

Defeating with the Truth, the Lord of Illusion
Bringing an end to this anaesthetising delusion.
Restoring Your reign right back to Earth —
People rejoicing, limbs full of mirth.
Souls singing at the top of their voice,
As their bodies, Spirits and Mind rejoices
At Your marvels in the end
When Your Holy of Holies You will send.
Upon Its silent transformative descent
Our Beings Enlightened, begin to Ascend.

* The devil (d*v*l) in this context relates to any entity of this dimension or any other, which breaks the Law of Love. It throws the Perfect Cosmic Order into chaos, fear, anger which cause suffering, anguish and pain. We are created to live in peace, unity, joy and harmony within the perfection of the Law of Love.

The Journey Must Go On

Continue to trust in who you are,
in God's Heart a precious Star
which shines ever so bright
filling Him-Her with great delight.
They bask in your radiance
and you rest in Their providence.

Continue to walk your path, albeit alone,
trudging along, dodging every stone
that in your path may lay,
your ardous journey waylay.
Keep walking ahead straight and tall,
even when evil knocks at your door!

For you are protected
your limbs injected
with a powerful strength
taking you to any length
wherever you need to go
We the way you will show.
You shall not hurt your feet
and evil, ye shall not defeat!

The path you shall have to walk
and the speech you shall have to talk
will all be Divinely inspired
as your Mind and Soul shall be rewired —
connected to the Great Mystery
as you carry out your most holy ministry.

Do not be afraid — do not fret,
Don't splash yourself with water and get wet!
Don't get your knickers in a twist
or do something silly like break a wrist.
Stay calm and still, collected and cool
Knowing yourself — your greatest tool!

And if they want to shut you down
and politely ask you to leave town
then say to them in no uncertain terms:
"I shall not go, you slimy worms.
I am here on a mission
to fulfil my Divine commission
and leave town I shall not,
be it cold, or be it hot!
Whether you like me, or if you don't
leave this town, I definitely won't!"

Confuddled at your newfound power,
they, your fiery, feisty soul seek to devour.
Your message they also seek to hide,
with comments unkind and somewhat snide.

Do not be afraid — do not fret,
Don't dive in a puddle and get wet!
Just don't forget Who you are,
that luminous, dazzling, bright shining Star
in the Heart of God's Truth abiding,
from Love, Light and Life not hiding.

Your Divine commission's coming soon
Listen carefully, one afternoon
as you bask in the sun's warm embrace
with God as One, full of His-Her Grace.
You shall be summoned, hear the call
to save humankind, so long after the fall
guiding them back
to the Heart of their Origin,
irrespective of race or of religion.

So get your feet ready
and your legs steady
to walk the walk

and talk the talk
to travel far
by bus, by car
to spill the beans
of heavenly Kings and Queens
waiting to welcome us all
as we hurriedly heed the call.
Going to the Divine palace
be not embarrassed
to party till the small hours
in gardens, overflowing with flowers
taking a walk by the waterfall,
or eating delicatessen in the hall
raising a glass of juice or two
one for me and one for you!

This invitation, the Good News is — is open to all -
Just heed the call, just heed the call, just heed the call.

Pack your suitcase
just in case
you have to travel far
or perhaps you'll stay put, just where you are!
Either way, be prepared to hear
the Divine message loud and clear,

albeit whispered softly by a breeze
asking you fear and the din to release
so that to the party you may go
and thoroughly enjoy the life-changing show.

Love

They rejected Him on that fateful day,
as determined they were come what may,
to do away with the Son of Man
mutilate and murder if they can.

The fateful fall of the whole generation
back from every region and every nation,
sadly let their God down big time
His Son they slipped into sh*tty slime
and was passed over to His foe
a brutal murder, He will know.

And the nation that Abraham and Sarah propagated,
on that day was relegated
down — into the pits of hell
as their soul to the D*v*l they sell.

The whole of the Heavens shuddered in fear,
Mother Mary, The Magdalene and John stayed very near
to the Son of God as He was condemned
and why, they could not comprehend.
How this nation who since a child They'd nursed,
the Son of the Hand that fed them in the desert, cursed.
Betrayed through lies, jealousy and deceit,

when miraculous Love had been His receipt
with which He'd gifted all those who came
the blind, the dumb, the sick and the lame
to be in their whole being healed
and God's Love in their own hearts sealed.

He taught them THE PEACEFUL WAY
so that they too, would one day
work miracles the same as He,
move mountains, walk across the sea.
But alas, the ending went all sour,
His precious Life ending prematurely
                God's own little flower.
This Son was born on Christmas Day
a testament of God's Love come what may.

Light

Acknowledge, embrace, proclaim the Light
Let it shine,
This Light Divine.
Do not stop it
keep it lit.
If, for some it shines too bright
And they cannot bear its light
Then let them walk away
And at a safe distant distance let them stay.

For some it shows a path
That they would like to take
But, due to fears make
A judgement call
Off the path to fall
Routed off their own right track
Instead of going forwards, going back!

Your Light reminds them of their fall
Of the peace and love that are no more
Of where they once had been before!
And as they are blinded,
Their lives' route rewound
stepping back

to where it's black!
Searching hither and thither, where
Hearts whither
Souls darken
Spirits die.
In that place
There is no light
In sight
Shining bright.

The darkness a veil of black lace
envelops their deepest, darkest place.
Your light disturbs their dark, deep pit
Which is full of fear as they sit
Wondering why your light them annoys
In a world of fear, full of noise.

They want to clamber back into the light,
Dispel their darkness, and it fight
Until it's gone and overcome
That might be the story for some.

Alas, for some others the dark stays black —
As they watch the aftermath of their own shipwreck!
The sturdy sides burst and crushed
Deep drowning waters in forcefully rushed

Sinking their ship deep
As their drowning souls weep.
It's not much fun
On the ocean floor,
Where the light, is light no more!

Is it too late, or are they in time?
Is the eleventh-hour still yet to chime?
Will they get out and themselves save,
or will their souls be swamped by waves
which their whole being seek to enslave?
Will they return safely to the top
and back themselves to upright prop?
Will they make it back to the light
if up they paddle with all their might?
Or is it too late, are they not in time?
Is it the twelfth hour's time now to chime?

Look and listen at every sign,
By God's grace and grand design
A message loud, a message clear:
"The End of Time approaching, near
have no fear, have no fear!"

Just paddle up back to the top
With power, strength and will — do not stop.

Just go back to the time of childhood
When innocence, faith and trust would
Lift you up, not take you down,
Make you smile and not make you frown.

You are still in time
For the twelfth chime's
Not gone, yet —
You can make it, I bet!

Get to the shore and slowly recover
your breath and gently rediscover
as you stop and on the sand pause
in the Here and Now not in what was.
In the here and now is the Grace
That will sweetly end the phase
Of going back and going forth
that place of darkness toward.

In the Here and Now is the Breath
In the Here and Now is the Truth
In the Here and Now is the Peace
In the Here and Now is the Bliss
In the Here and Now is the Joy
In the Here and Now is the Love
In the Here and Now is the Light

In the Here and Now is the Life
In the Here and Now is Infinity
In the Here and Now is Eternity.

Come and sit
It's all well lit
In the Present
Of the Presence
Of God's embrace
Full of Divine grace.
In the Truth
Of your Being
Rest tranquil
And sit still
Rest in the Knowing.

God's waiting
Love's gracing
Your way back.
Despite the crash
Despite the dark
In spite of the din
Despite drowning
He'll take you back, go
He'll take you back, so
Together with Him you shall live

In His Love and grace.
Moving
Resting
Breathing.
We are One.

Life

It's been a long saga of torture and pain,
Left everybody changed, never the same.
Hearts died
anguish'd, abide'd
where Life hid.
Then Love amid
the anguish melted
the agony belted
away the Heart
full of Grief.

Alas, the bloody murder and death!
Glorified by some
killed also His mum.
After three days His Heavenly Being's restored
to the Heavens lifted and adored.
The pain did silently seep
into the wooden bars as they weep
for the evil that took hold of that day
determined to destroy the Son of God, come what may.

He suffered over the years,
in the Heavens shed His tears
over souls that were lost, hearts

of hard cold metal and steel darts
speared through His heart to its core.
Sadly, Love and Life they shall know, no more.

But, He looked at them lovingly
and showered them with peace, love and mercy
quenching their thirst
with a Love that will burst.
Asking them to come back home to his gentle loving heart
so that of Him and His limitless Love they are always a part.

But sadly, they turned their hearts away,
Nothing their allegiance to the B**st could sway.
They had vouched their hearts wholly to him
everyday acting out a brand-new sin.
All the time rejecting God's Light
shunning His Love, rejecting Delight.
It saddened the Son
and even His mum,
that all that agony and pain,
may have even been in vain.

Their hearts had closed,
and souls had darkened.

Beings locked in their own prison cell
endorsing fear and anger with every knell
embracing fear's and anger's ringing bell.
Rejecting The Son and His way of Life
freeing from fear, slavery, and strife.

The freedom that He came to bring,
a few faithful souls of this did sing.
Their hearts and souls with joy now ring,
the Ones who wholeheartedly loved the Son,
although He'd hoped it'd be everyone.
They sang of His Glory through day and night
gathering crowds, a glorious sight.
They would shout out from the top of the hills,
their voices ringing through doors and window sills.
For, no amount of evil kills
that Love for Him, their whole heart fills.
They come to the Son, they come to Him
With their empty cups, now overflowing —
their eyes and faces presently a-glowing
with His gentle and loving Grace
raining over the human race.

Now His own all welcome Him back
in their hearts abundant Love, not lack
of love, peace, joy and light

in their hearts and beyond, shining bright.
He comes His own to gather and be,
with His beloveds through Eternity.

The Presence

My heart aches as I leave my sons at home,
as I heed the Call of the Isle of Avalon.
Let me, let go of my attachment to them,
to set them free, as I did You back then.
To let God have the fruit of my womb
whether in a stable, a house or a tomb.
God resurrects the fruit of my loins,
back to Him He gathers my boys.
He loves how freely I give and offer up His Own —
allowing Him to have all of our beings, down to the
bone!
For myself, the grace of God and His favour suffices,
Revealing Himself through mysterious devices.
I know His peace in my heart,
What shall I say, where do I start?
The peace He gives is subtle and sweet,
Where Love, Joy and Sweetness meet.
He blesses me with His Divine Spirit
fills me with His grace beyond limit
for His love for me and for us all,
I leave everything and heed the Call.

Do not dawdle, please get going,
The Son you the way now is showing.

Don't waste time on looking back,
walk briskly, forge straight ahead.
He's the Way to be walked,
He's the Word to be taught.
He's here for you,
can you be here, too?

He'll whisper sweet nothings of Love in your ear
continuously His sweet music in your ear you'll hear.
You'll feel His Presence strengthen your bones
His Power, His Strength heighten the tones
of the sweet music that He plays on your heart-strings
Gently, sweetly, softly His Love sings.
Alas, let go of all you attach to
walking the way, as you choose to do.
Be fearless, shameless, pure and true
and love Him dearly as He loves you!

Surrendering

May Your Holy Will be done in me,
for Your Glory all the Earth to see.
As You have saved your mum
You've come to save everyone.

So that free from anguish, pain and fear,
Love, Peace and Joy can be Here -
through Your beloved people of Light,
always with Your Law of Love in sight.
Shining Your sweet Love so pure and true
their hearts, mind, bodies and souls renew.
A new Heaven and a new Earth abound,
Listen carefully... sssssshhhhh... you can hear its sound!
Springing forth within each Light-worker,
each humble and true life searcher.
Truth Divine and Justice restored,
as the days of old, God's Law adored.
A new creation, starting anew
for everyone, not just a few
Love its brand new currency
Light as a matter of urgency
Life according to God's sweet plan
it's how they'll live, God's brand new clan.

His community, His people, His true ones.
They start again, dads, children and mums
living on the Earth secure,
Fear of Death, not anymore!
Only peace in their hearts and on the land,
in every seed, in every grain of sand.

Love's Reassuring Words

When demons wage their deadly war on you
as they presently are and always prone to do,
Don't get despondent and don't feel sad,
don't allow yourself to feel beaten and bad.

They come to tempt and lure in the pure,
their peace and light for themselves to secure.
Procuring respite, claiming the light as their own,
for the darkness which they themselves have sown
envelops their whole being —
for the darkest Darkness is what they sow,
and the darkness of the Darkest is what they know.

So when Beings of Light
take flight
and shine bright
the Dark ones come to prowl,
with their fangs slimy scowl,
Sowing fear, anger and pain
seeking the Light Beings' light to gain.
The pure Light Beings are unaffected
true to their Truth and Heart they stay,
keeping the Darkest darkness away.
Do know, that the purer the soul does shine,

with Love sublime and Light Divine,
the more the Darkness does attack
to take their light and peace, for their lack
of light and peace and love is maddening,
and their state of being is sorely saddening.

So when they whisper words of fear,
doubt, guilt, shame, anguish, My Dear —
know that I am Here
and your pleas for help, I do hear.
My Presence strengthens and enlivens,
The Spark of Love which in you lives.

The Calming of the Storm

A terrible storm rages outside.
The wind howling through the trees
rattling my bones, shaking my knees.
Reminding me of a time gone by
when sleeping in a boat we lie.
The waves crashed against the prow
mentally torturing my brain, contorting my brow-
Would we make it safely to the shore?
Rudely awakened, I'm not sure.
I look at Him and say no word
to stop the storm, is that absurd?
Our eyes meet and in a split second
my whole life in my head, I amend.
Will we live, or will we die
beneath the ocean floor to lie?

He looks at me back, eyes serene
What does that calm, reassuring gaze mean?
Does it mean we shall be spared?
Is it possible that He dost know
what His words do not show?
His tall, strong countenance calm, serene

in that storm, weather extreme.
Boat rocking violently from side to side
how can He so still abide?
We'll all be lost, we shan't be found
hit by waves of fear and doubt profound.
The mental anguish and the pain
hit the boat, like nails of rain.
Will we capsize
or will He realise?

He is the Lord of all the storms
His powers beyond Nature and its norms
He calms the storm. With a loud, stern command
the wind subsides at the resonance and sound
thundering through the crashing waves
the storm subsides. Our lives He saves.
A single blow, just one loud order
the wind dies down
the howling sound
the crashing waves
just simply, stop.

Calm ensued
Spirits renewed

boat recalibrated
storm liberated.
Clouds shift
Waters sift
back into the sea.
Boat slowly steadies
rocking to and fro
waters aboard throw.

Safely we reach the shore
Fear and doubt are no more.
He chides us for our lack of faith
and laughs as we are now safe.
For the same as He calms down the storm
we also could do that since we were born.
But, our power we have sadly lost
amidst conditioning, brainwashing — at a great cost.
As when storms hit us now and here
our own inner voice loud and clear
has the power the storm to dissipate
Mother Nature and us amalgamate.
We like Him too, storms can subside
If only we remembered! If only we recall
then storms in our lives, will be storms no more.

Reclaim your power that is Within You
has been and will always be —
to heal, make whole and renew
tempestuous storms to subdue
Evil to eliminate
Fear to dissipate.

The Sound Summons

My Spirit overflows with Your sweet Presence
and my whole being reveberates with Your pure Essence
sitting in Your Holy Space
with Your most Holy Sound Nada me to embrace.

If only all were aware of Your Presence
feeling Your pure, Divine Essence,
reveberating in the depths of their Being,
knowing, feeling and hearing what their eyes aren't
seeing!

Perhaps, if you whispered softly, through
the gentle, sensous caressing breeze to
sing in their ears a sweet melody
each of their own incredible beauty?

Or if you shouted out aloud,
with bolts of lightning through a thunder cloud
and told them in no uncertain terms
that they really belong to the Heavenly Realms?

What if your song through waves resounds,
bringing to their ears those Heavenly sounds
notes unsurpassed, unplayed ever before,

sweet, soft symphonies and much much more?

Would they listen, would they tune in
to the live music playing within?
Telling them of their true Divine nature,
not to be attached to their flighty physical stature
as it wilts and dies this transitional bodily form,
that unfortunately is at the moment, the norm!

So, instead of building temples of stone,
why don't you come to God alone,
in the living temple of your heart
God's own creation, His own work of art
singing His Glory with songs of praise,
Listening to God's own celestial sound and see what it
says?

VOLUME III

Mother and Son Reunited their Love Reignited I

'Mary, Go... Go... Go...
We go with you, so
Do not worry or be scared
All your prayers shall be heard.'

And know that the Love between Mother and Son,
Is the Love with which He Loves everyone.
Wherever you are, whatever you do,
know and feel in your heart that He loves you too.

Let these few verses inspire you to see,
His infinite Love for you and for me.
Whoever you are, wherever you may be
experience for yourself and examine carefully.
See if it resonates inside you wholly
Don't take my word for it, go that extra mile
to test it for yourself
take your time, be patient
it may take a while!

Mother and Son Reunited and their Love Reignited II

Where would you like me to be Son, what would You
have me do?
My heart beats loudly with love for You.
As when I stood under that damn'd cross
Your Father's handmaid — He is the boss!

I offer up lovingly my life and my light,
praying that in my being, He may find delight.
Praying that every prayer muttered,
that every praise uttered,
that every meditation and song
may to the Godhead belong.

Coming forth once more-
Slowly, yet surely opening the door
allowing God's Law and Divine Will
to fill my whole being, until
once again, I know His Presence
deep within me — my Essence.

I love my Son, I love Him dearly
I lost Him once and again nearly.
Hence, the dreams of losing Dan

looking back and thinking when
those dreams came as a warning sign
part of God's almighty grand design.
To get me back home to my Son Divine through dreams,
which I at the time misunderstood, it seems.

I very nearly lost my chance.
Yet, a gentle nudge and a diddy dance,
from the Heavens in my Heart
following the thread
the signs it read
of what I must do
where I must go
who I must see
for to Truth and Love faithful be.

By God's pure grace and Love unending
My story's not ended in despair never-ending
for He has turned my homecoming
into a lush feast of a prodigal daughter becoming.
And like the Prodigal Son when he came back,
He hugged and kissed me and cut me some slack!
So overjoyed at my return, the Heavens burst
with joy!
So now Love, Peace, Joy and Harmony,
me always silently accompany

everywhere I go, whatever I do
They are there and so is He too.
I realise now that the past is gone, done and dusted!
God's own Love and grace my sin has busted.
I am so happy and finally at peace,
my karmic debt and wretchedness released.
I can't believe my luck
as out of the pit, unstuck
and free to roam the Earth with glee
that was created for you and for me.

To walk once again with my Son
reunited now — we are One.
Never to be apart ever again,
always together come what may.
Through tears and laughter, sadness and mirth
through resurrection and a new birth.
Overcoming murder by the knife
coming back fully alive to Life.

As Mother and Son reunite
the Mother's love reignite
The Son's jumping over the moon
Coming back in Glory very soon
To His Mother and to all His lambs and sheep
in His Father's sheepfold to keep

safe, from harm's way
never again to be taken away.
All come together united in the Law
the Law of Love as He always foresaw.

And His own Beloveds with them to dine -
on Heavenly manna, as they shine
brighter than stars and suns
where forever fresh water runs.
They shine and shimmer in the Infinite Garden of
Mystery
an epic end to a very long story.
A happy ending all around
the music of angels making a joyful sound.
Welcoming the throngs to the Heavenly place,
people coming from every country and every race
the gates wide open
the windows too
be guided in and follow
the King of Kings, hereto.

The Music it plays
the Peace it stays,
the Perfume it smells
of Love it tells!
The Laughter it rings,

of harmony it sings
The Rejoicing it springs
with angelic wings.
The mansion is filling
with those who are willing
to come back to Love and Light
to the Heavenly Father-Mother's delight.

Music plays
Hips sway
Dancing forever
from God never
to be separated
the union amalgamated.
Now always as One
as the course of time will run
an Eternity of bliss
Earth and Heaven kiss
as Beings are adoring
their Godhead's praise soaring
High into His-Her ears
With a multitude of cheers.
A final reunion,
An end to delusion,
And an end to suffering and pain.
An end to anger

An end to fear
An end to violence
An end to jealousy
An end to envy
An end to poverty
An end to hate
An end to greed
An end to lust
An end to injustice
An end to prejudice
An end to war
An end to how things are.

As a new Dawn dawns, verily
Peace, love, joy, togetherness in unity.
Safe and free from fear,
Living in God, His voice hear.
His Love feel enfolding your heart,
You've made it home, never depart!
Stay with Him in His Holy Law,
Which wipes away every flaw.

And as the Father-Mother loves the Son
He-She has always loved everyone!
Come now, without further ado
Do your laces, buckle your shoe.

Hurry! Time's of the essence, move
Go to your Heavenly haven, fear remove.
Full of God, of His Love and Light
rest, sleep and have a "good night"
sleep tight.
Now rest in the fact we are all One
Father-Mother, us and the Son.

Michael Mother and Son

I climbed up the hill albeit at one point in time got
stuck
halfway up.
Do I continue to climb
or do I descend and decline?
I bit the bullet and clambered up
in spite of the path being slippery with mud.
And to my utter and sheer surprise
arrived the back way to the rise
of the tor from the side,
where the path was very narrow, not wide.

I felt within the soles of my feet,
as I stood where the Mary and the Michael lines meet
A strange sensation, a pacifying peace
a new life arising, on life a new lease!
A joy arising
as peace abiding
a freedom true
Love to imbue

In the soles of my feet where the Mary and the
Michael lines meet.
I looked around
as a melodious sound
rang in my ears
singing away my fears.
A red rose petal I found
as velvety and as smooth as the sound
that reverberated through the soles of my feet
where the Mary and the Michael lines meet.

I, Mary climbed up and as I landed
a beautiful presence on me descended.
The Lord Mikaal, or Michael to you,
came to me welcome and to greet me, too.
"I've been waiting Mariya,
I've been waiting for you,
You were brought to the tor
to meet me, for
Here Your Beautiful Beloved Son walked
the hills listened as He talked.
Birds sang their simple song
it was perfect then, with nothing wrong."
I felt the warm welcome in the soles of my feet,

where the Mary and the Michael lines meet.

"I, Lord Mikaal or Michael as you will,
have walked with you and walk with you still.
My aim you and Your Son to be reunited
And for your love for Him to be reignited
On His favourite spot of all time
He shall make your whole being shine."
And a luminous Light shone around the soles of my
feet,
where the Mary and the Michael lines meet.

My Being rejoices at the presence of my Son,
the Son of God, the most Holy One.
And most grateful and thankful am I
That you, Mikaal, have not passed me by.
But, brought me back to my Beloved Son
so that now we can all be One.
"On the hill He too had walked," the Hill declared to
the soles of my feet,
there, just where the Mary and the Michael lines meet.

"I must now depart, Mariya, my dearest soul,
as I have gladly achieved my desired goal.

Mother and Son are finally reunited
their Love for each other is now reignited.
The bond is strong and tested, too
You Love Him and He loves you,"
softly whispered Lord Mikaal to the soles of my feet,
and the message ran throughout my Being to greet
the land where the Mary and the Michael lines meet.

The Birth

You held your Baby, you held Him tight,
You kissed and cuddled Him right through the night
Your heartbeat overflowing with Love, His rest
All had been accomplished, Mary, you'd passed the test.

He rested His tiny head on your warm-loving chest,
And suckled silently on your tiny breast.
Peace enveloped you and Him, and all around
choirs of angels singing, the only sound.

A stillness, a tranquillity, a peace of Heaven in the stable
And Mary, Joseph, shepherds and animals were able
to acknowledge that the Son of God is born
A new way to live He gives, a brand new Dawn.

The cow and the donkey and the sheep
Are so proud Him to meet and greet!
Lowly stable animals, in a humble abode
Just as the angels said and the Prophecy foretold.
The Star shone bright
The Baby in sight
Illuminating His face
is Divine Grace
His whole Being to embrace.

Into the Light
God's own Heart's delight
Shining and cutting through Dark —
a contrast deep, so stark.
A warmth ensues
the cold subdues
the Baby rests
in linen vests
Wrapped up tight
through that sweet night.

The Mother goes to Bethlehem (on the Feast of the Immaculate Conception)

I held Him tight, close to my chest,
as He drank milk from my tiny breast
my heart with a joy and love over-flowing
as the stable with the star's lights a-glowing.
A deep peace, envelops the cave
as God to humanity His only Son gave.

Stillness, as the shepherds adored,
Glory as the peace'd been restored.
Heaven has come down to Earth to
show the way of Love and Freedom to me and to you.
The shepherds and their faithful sheep
warm peace in the stillness did keep.

And as He nestled to my breast,
Him and I and all the rest
felt Heaven's door open wide
Their Presence with the Son reside.
He suckled slowly, His first earthly meal,
His humanity, the Son of God did seal.

I looked at Him, in wonder and awe,
My heart rejoicing, at what my eyes saw

My heart warm, as he fed on milk raw.
My hands held Him tight,
for He is the Light,
for all of us to follow,
today and tomorrow.
The Son of God, this little babe
Of Love and Life and Light is made,
will one day show all the Way,
and to all one day He will say:

"Listen to My words, I speak the Truth of God.
My Father in Heaven loves you dearly,
His heart over-flowing to the brim and clearly
wants you ALL to come back home to The Heavenly
Estate
I tell you all this, on His mandate.
So, that where I am then you are too,
You all can come, be there, YES YOU!
All of your heart, mind, soul and body,
tall, short, fat, slim, dark, fair, everybody.
Come back to the Heart of God supreme
and with His-Her golden grace let your whole Being
beam.
I will show you all how
We'll all find a way, somehow!
I'll make it easy, as you just follow Me

then the Way, you'll clearly see.
The blindness from your eyes disappears
and clarity, insight, intuition reappears.
You will be renewed and born once more
so to enjoy the Grace of God and Him adore."

And, I, His Mother on Earth did ponder,
these events in awe and wonder
as Heaven's Son in my arms did lay,
keeping him safe come what may.
My heart aglow with Love Divine
for my God and for this Son of mine.

So grateful for Joseph's presence, too as he
is forgotten, oftentimes in the whole story, you see!
His firm, faithful presence did us strengthen
throughout his life I do need to mention.
He stayed honest, fair, loving and true
Loving the Son of God and in Him imbue
a love for the skill of working with wood,
beautiful carvings his hand could
wield. He taught the Son this trade,
so He too, beautiful carvings made.

In the stable Joseph stayed,
And on him my head I laid.

As he beheld the Son and His mum,
it's like he beheld everyone,
who would welcome The Son of the Most High
and in His Law of Love rest, nigh!

Humble, yet firm,
Gentle and sweet —
Here's where Heaven and Earth meet.
In this stable in a cave,
The Son of God, His Life He gave,
for on His Birthday celebrated,
is the Earth's balance recalibrated.

As the portals to the Heavens opened wide,
so that humanity may no longer hide
in hatred, anger, and in fear
resting only in Love, Light and Life, as God is here!

Mother, Son and Everyone

Mother and Son reunited
their love for each other reignited,
Always there, but by sin obscured
now it's shining bright, fully renewed.
His Heart is full and overflowing
Her heart rejoices in the knowing
that He is here.
To Him she joyously clings
as her Soul His praises sings.
She is overjoyed at the prospect
that now her soul He will protect
from untruths, false dogmas and doctrines.
The Truth shall set her free
and not just her, but everybody.

And her whole Being remembers clearly
When He as a child would wander freely
into woods and climb up trees
into rivers up to his knees
cheekily grinning, full of life
free from worry, free from strife.
She would hold him close to her
hug him, teach him not to err.
A great teacher was she

and a great one will always be.

He, a great Son
second to none.
Loving all dearly
unto death clearly.
All sins forgiven
Atoned, absolved, forgotten
His Love
above
and beyond all their din
His grace above and beyond all their sin.
Their anointment's already taken place
it will redeem her and the whole human race.
Redemption will come to all very soon
with a banging whish and a whopping boom!

The world awaits patiently and with joyous anticipation
As the crown of our own reparation
is gifted from the Heavens above
renewing what has been smashed, restoring hopes that
had been crushed —
filling the whole Earth below and above with His
sublime, unconditional Love.

The Two Mothers

This is the humble mother of Your Son when on Earth,
sharing Motherhood with the Divine Earth and Her
hearth.
Both Mothers' hearts overflowing with love for their
Dearly Beloved Son
both Mothers' love pure, supreme second to none.
Both Mothers supporting Him as His Divine plan did
unfold,
a lot of these stories are still left hidden, untold!
The rapturous joy at His birth they both felt
and in deep adoration, both of them knelt.
A deep peace enveloped both Mary and Aurora Divine
as in unison they both sang: "He is not mine,
but belongs to the Godhead up above and below
as to the people, God's Love He must show."
And although through Mary He came and He stayed,
both her and His Divine Earthly Mother on Earth he
obeyed.
Her angels surrounded both Him and her
And for them all, the angels did care.

Aurora Divine watched with joy and with glee
Mary's love for their Yeshua, she did clearly see.
A love deep, touching, sweet-smelling of roses,

a love although strong, yet as delicate as posies.
And Aurora relished the fun that was had,
on sweet summer nights when their hearts were so glad.
Mother Mary sweet stories, her Yeshua she told
and He listened transfixed, as of heroes so bold
who fought without fear, to bring justice and peace
the baddies to get rid of, the goodies to release!
Stories of heroes who in love for their Creator,
embraced, accepted and proclaimed Him as their Maker.
And the Son intently listened to His sweet Mother's
tales,
such lessons of God's Love for males and females,
for tall, short, fat, dark or fair
for strong, weak and those in disrepair.

Mother Aurora watched as Mary taught Him to pray-
to trust in His Father-Mother Divine come what may.
He loved her prayers, the Sweet Son of God
He listened intently, silently relishing
Her company cherishing
Her motherhood adoring
as prayers come pouring
forth.

They joked, laughed, played and had fun,
Love shone brightly from Mother to Son.

The Son Himself, her He adored,
in Mary's heart these stories still stored.
Queen Aurora watched the two together
both their hearts fluttering as light as feather
running, jumping and skipping around,
their laughter the most joyful sound
To Queen Aurora's ears
these two dearly Beloved Dears
brought Her joy and made life sweet.
At dawn Her angels did both meet
with blessings true, the day to greet
with a sweet mornings dew and other blessings too!

The angels by day joined in the fun,
as He toddled around, His walking'd begun.
They sang their hearts out, Him and Mary sweet
the day with delicious music did each of them greet!

The Son to His Mother I

Mother, Mother let me whisper in your ear,
Dearest Mother know that I am here.
I love you dearest with a Love so sublime
and care for your being with a kindness Divine.
No Mother is greater, than this Mother of mine.

She sang to me sweetly when I was just a babe
gurgling sweet noises of joy I had made.
How we played together and what fun we had
albeit, sometimes it was hard and quite sad
as we suffered poverty, were outcasts, ostracised, it is
said.

Her sweet-smelling smile an exquisite perfume
You'd always smell her aura when she entered a room.
Her sweetness abided not just for me
She was so generous, sweet and all could see
She was the best mother, she could ever be.

She tended me gently, with compassionate care
nobody would hurt me, nobody would dare,
as she'd come charging at them like an angry bull
With a bucket of cold water full.
Her protective love and kindness so beautiful.

The Son to His Mother II

You have been focused too much on your earthly sons
then,
and yet, your Jesus is now a fully grown man.
He's been trying to get you back to Him
free from fear, anguish and the din.
His infinite longing's been to be reunited,
and your love for Him to be reignited,
so that like the days of old,
as the story has been told
you are close together once again One
The loving, dear Mother and her Dearly Beloved Son.
I've waited for many years
and shed quite a many tears
as you mum did not heed the call,
as if you didn't care at all!
You denied your inner Truth
a grief took hold of me, a sadness untold.

Until you quickly clambered through the back gate
almost, almost a bit too late!
You almost missed the boat that sailed,
and I Myself to get you back had almost failed.
Yet, the boat you did not miss, but got
on just in time, missed it not!

And once aboard, you prayed and prayed
Petitions of Love to your Creator relayed.
Your homecoming to Me and to yourself celebrated,
a return so long-awaited.
Joy beyond words filled My heart,
coupled with a promise to never depart.
I'd hoped and waited you would return
And leave the dusty, desolate roads you did sojourn.

I know you love Me, mumsie dear
this to Me is ever so clear.
Your life you have now turned around.
Helped by Nada, that Heavenly sound
as the melodious music of the Universe grew,
leading you back home to the Love within you once
knew.
And once back home to Me within, you came
then nothing, nothing stayed the same!
I changed and you transformed
heart, mind, body and soul reformed.
I rejoice in your new birth,
We celebrate here, full of mirth.
A new Mary, a new mum to Me,
a new Virgin Mother for all to see.

I'm so glad and overjoyed

dancing, skipping, springing, the return enjoyed!
And now, mumsie dear it's getting late,
and it'll be soon time to open the gate
to the dream world, and rest your sweet head,
on a soft pillow, no tears to shed!
In your dreams I shall come
I'll come to you mum.
So that you can recall
the teachings of old and much, much more!
You'll know what to do,
where to go,
what to say —
My Spirit goes in front, before and ahead
for 'I AM The Way' as I said.
So, saunter ahead tall and straight
and this time, please, please don't be late!
Get on the boat and sail with Me,
across the rivers and walk on the sea.

The Son to His Mother III

Mother, release that anger, anguish, agony and pain,
My Calvary will never be in vain!
The hammer's down, the nails are in
To free each and every one from sin.
I lay there, so meek and so lame,
Taking on Humanity's shame.

The Father-Mother and the Holy One look on,
They do love Him, They love the Son.
Yet, the soul-contract I have signed,
The whole of Calvary pre-designed.
Could it have been avoided that treacherous murder?
But, die I did, that is for sure
the b**st and his hell took me to the floor.

Yet now I am alive. I live once more,
I wipe away what was before!
A new shoot springs, a fresh new start
God's very own renewed work of art.
A new Earth for you and them to enjoy
Freedom, love, peace and joy.

To you, dearest Mother, I say these words
I protect and provide as I do these flocks of birds.

To you, dearest Mother, who has loved me so,
I apologise for I had to go —
Not in a way a Mother would dream,
That the life of her Son so meaningless would seem.
I am sorry, my dearest Mother, so true,
that as I died on the cross so did you.
I made you suffer, in silence and pain,
So that your life was never the same.
I am sorry that your heart so pure,
Beyond breaking point had to endure.
An agony that would rip your heart apart
A shooting pain right through your Mother's heart!
It left you searching, finding a way
To let the pain go, sometimes going astray.
Trying to find meaning in it all,
Spending lifetimes heeding the call
Of trying to bring all souls to me
So that the fruits of our agony
Would not in vain or pointless be.
It enlarged your heart, expanded your soul
a mission to heal yourself, became your goal.
A pain that into love transforms
All the pain and all the thorns
Defies how much a person can endure
In heart, mind, body never secure.
Your heart, it yearns to be set free

It yearns for peace and tranquillity
Filled with love for all humanity."
With much love,
Your Son.

The Heavenly Father to the Virgin Mother

Dearest Mary,
I'm so sorry too — please know this, please, please do!
I didn't know it would kill you all
that nasty murder, that treacherous fall.
It's taken far too long to heal,
the restoration, the brand-new seal
to be allowed to stamp Creation
on the Heart of every nation!
And yet now He is Risen
out of the humanly and earthly prison.
He is fully restored
in Hearts adored.
Pure Essence of Life, Love and Light
Full of power, compassion and might.
His Living presence in those who love Him
Frees them from Fear itself and from fear of Death.
His Living presence in those who don't
wants to shine forth, but if it's blocked it won't!

The murder from long ago now forgotten,
A new reality's now begotten.
Still some work needs to be done,
So many more to Love still needing to come.

Your son, he suffers no more
as many more still come through the door.
To come and enjoy the sumptuous feast
from the very most to the very least
all are invited. Some decline,
some are busy, some come to dine.

Mother and Son —
A Dialogue

"You are here, mumsie, dear
That to Me is now so clear.
Rest your weary head on my chest,
that's it, great! Get some rest
from that wretchedness that demons lay in your path,
Leaving a dark and painful aftermath.
Rest your weary soul, my mum,
I'll let you know, this is your Son.
Leave the wretchedness and please do come
rest in My heart, as we are now One."
(The Son to His mum)

"I can feel your gentle heartbeat,
as my head and Your heart meet.
I can hear the Nada sound
throughout my mind, body and soul resound.
I'm glad to rest in Your peace supreme
As You, with Your Love, myself redeem."
(The Mother to the Son)

"As in the days of old
I am being told,
When I a tiny babe in your loving arms

You held me tightly out of harm's
way, and you steered all darkness away.
And as I had rested my tiny ear,
on your chest I too, could hear
the gentle rhythm of your love playing
as a Joy, Kindness and Peace saying
that you, Mother, Mother of mine
loved Me then and now with a love Divine.

The past wretchedness gone and buried,
beautiful memories of our love untarried.
When two thousand years ago,
Your love in earthly way did show.
And here now two thousand years after,
Your love surpassed Death, alive ever-after.
It survived all the traps that'd been laid
to trip you up, your path to Me waylaid.
Stopping you from coming back
dumping you into a deep, dark sack.
And because of the darkness and despair in there
you wouldn't be able to go anywhere.
They laid traps, but didn't see
the formidable love you have for Me.
Let's not worry 'bout what went on before.
What's done, is done and now over,
Your virtue shaped like a four-leaved clover,

compassion, kindness, love and a generous heart,
as Your Devotion sings "How Great Thou art".
(The Son to His mum)

"U Superjur and mum and Nanna Nina
Ikollkom ħniena minna, itolbu għalina.
Kunu miegħi f'dal-ġranet li ġejjin,
tgħidulix li intom għajjenin!
Ejjew bi ħġarkom, għinuni f'li gej
bi grazzji, kuraġġ u l-paċi tal-Feddej.
Mank nista' narakom, naqra zgħira,
immiskom
inxommkom
inħosskom, dażgur.
Kif intom m' Ibni ta' Alla l-Maħtur,
tħossuH, tarawH u tkellmuH.
Kemm hi safja dik ir-ruħ,
illi Lilu tħoss fil-fond tal-qalb,
u Lilu tkellem dejjem fit-talb.
Inħobbu lil Ibni, ta' Alla l-Maħtur,
Imżejjen bil-Glorja ta' Salvatur.
Inħobbu lil Ibni b'imħabba tal-ġenn,
U l-imħabba Tiegħu għalija dejjem hi kenn.
Mhux li kien inħossu f'dirgħajja
bhal fl-ewwel Milied, meta gew ir-rgħajja,
u rawH fuq sidri jistrieħ,

jiekol u jixrob qatiegħ
ħalli guħ u għatx ma jbatix.
L-imħabba tiegħi bħal għarix
ittieh kenn mill-bard ta' barra,
kenn mill-qalb li minn ALLA tiżgarra
kenn mill-ħruxija tal-qlub magħluqin
offrulu mħabba safja, bhal ikel bnin."

The Channelling bursts into the Maltese language still expressing her love for her SON hoping it offers Him solace and warmth. Protecting Him not just from the cold in the cave in Bethlehem, but from cold hearts that do not want to know Him and His Love. The Mother urges everybody to offer their pure love as a wholesome offering like that of a pure meal.

Mother to Son

I am grateful beyond words
for I am back home where I belong,
sorry Son it's taken so long.
But the plan is now being fulfilled
as my homecoming with joy is filled
may it benefit everyone,
Humanity, me and our heavenly plans, my Son.

I'm so delighted to wake up and see
that really You've never left me.
But, due to the agony I lost my path
the sad outcome of its aftermath.
I was never able to be the same
Yet, Your love within me will always remain.
The anguish melts
The pain like rain
falls, to my soul calls
allowing it to be reformed
into Love transformed.
Your presence in me now fulfilled
the raging storm presently stilled.

My Son arisen. My Son alive.
A Son whose Love for all is beyond measure —

whose presence in one's heart — an eternal treasure
of peace and joy, beyond any price
Our Lord Yeshua, Jesias, Jesus The Christ.

VOLUME IV

Back Home, Where We Belong!

Back Home where we belong,
Hymns of praise are our song
peace, love and joy abound
at Love's calling, a silent sound.
In our Hearts and in the eye of our mind we can see
Clearly, His Love, Light and Life within you and me!
A New Heaven, a New Earth
is now being given birth.

The One in All, the All in One

Rose incense wending its way to me,
so that where You are, so shall I be.
Specks of dust dancing in the light,
frivolous, free fairies twirling in delight!

They come to greet me and whisper softly:
"Hi Mary, welcome home
to your Divine Heavenly throne.
Not of the human earthly plane
but, in the Heights of Heaven, let me explain!
Within the inner world deep in the heart,
it represents… Um… where shall I start?
The Essence from which all Life emerges
where love, light and life converges.
Within that expansive, boundary-free space
abides the whole of the human race.
And not just that, but all creation too
including all, and me and you!

A whole universe is the earthly human heart,
where all is one, as all is part
of the One bigger whole,
to experience this is each soul's goal.
It's not a seeing through our human sight.

No, it's a Knowing of the Light
through the third eye on the forehead
you see what the naked eye can't get!

The heart begins to glow with such warmth and peace
through the chambers of the heart like a waterfall
flowing
glistening with its Peace and Knowing
doubt's destroyed as insight grows
Heart, Body and Mind this Truth upholds.

The Spirit within the Heart and Mind,
when this Essence inside they finally find
leap up for joy and open wide
putting fear, anger, shame and guilt aside.
They twirl and swirl Body, Heart, Spirit and Mind —
a Dance of Unity — as One.

The Breath joins in
to expand within
that Universe
so enthrallingly diverse
so pure and deep
where angels keep
their secrets sweet.
Spirit abides

not hides,
in the depths of each soul,
part of the Whole
ALL IS ONE!

The Body an Illusion creates,
which throughout heart and mind permeates
an illusion of division,
our perception needs revision.
That, that out there
is separate to that in him or her!
It is all one and transcends
body, and on our true seeing depends.
And through the body like a filter
the Spirit within and without infiltrate
and unite through the body's body
the Spirit within and without to embody.
No, it's not just in here, it's not just out there —
IT is in Everyone and Everywhere!

As Illusions drop
deceptions stop.
We know we are ONE,
Heart, Mind, Body, Breath, Father-Mother and the Son.

A New Heaven, A New Earth

Soon He comes to gather His nation, His Beloved Souls,
from east, west, north, south they assemble
as part of the Beloved Sons' ensemble.
Love and Life are the seeds He generously sows,
as abundant Love and Life on Earth grows.
The weeds that desecrate the garden floor,
must transform and be weeds no more!
They come straight out of the gentle ground,
with a loud lament and sickening sighing sound!
The flowers, fragrant, full of Life and Light
that throughout the years were His Heart's Delight
Are gently and carefully tended in the garden
of which He now is the most gracious warden.
A garden delightful, a garden perfect
everybody's pure, full of Love, Life, Light and respect.
The grass is lush green as never before seen
dazzling green blades with a bright silvery sheen
that fills the whole of the garden floor
as deep pink roses adorn the open door.
Through which they enter, joyfully come,
Each and Everyone!
Trees in blossom, red, blue, white, yellow, green
radiant rubies, dazzling diamonds, glistening gems
gleam.

They dance to the music of their gentle Lord
every leaf, branch, trunk, flower adored,
the resplendent life of the Godhead
Its creation, Its own vibrant bed.
Wherein now the peacemakers and the meek rest,
having journeyed to their own pre-prepared feathered
nest.
He welcomes them anew,
whether many or just a few,
who make it through the garden door
songs of praise on their lips,
as their God they lovingly adore.
They dance for joy, with ecstacy leap
As Oneness with their God they keep.
The water shimmers silver and gold
The Water of Life, they are told.
For them to bathe in day and night,
making their beings shine ever so bright.
The birds all sing a welcoming song -
Everything's perfect — there's nothing wrong!
A radiant blue bird with golden wings,
Songs of praise to God, it sings.
A thanksgiving gift to its Creator
an act of perfect adoration to its Maker.
A perfect pink rose joins in the hymn of praise
to all the newcomers to welcome and amaze.

All are in Communion Divine and perfect peace
the newcomers, the birds, herons and geese.
All living as One in harmony
all living as One happy family.
All living in God and His-Her Heavenly Kingdom,
partaking of His-Her Love, Life, Light and Wisdom.
The past is past, gone and forgotten.
A new Heaven on a new Earth is now begotten.
These faithful souls, these pure of heart
always a part of the Godhead art.

Hallelujah

Jesus has won, Well done Son! I knew it is done.
Your passion hasn't been in vain
as God's grace a refreshing rain
falls on the whole Earth and those returning to Grace -
quite a lot of the human race!

Enough to make it all worthwhile
making the Hosts of Heaven smile.
Enough to deck the halls with guests
who dine and shine as their weary hearts, rest.

A day of great grace all around,
the new Jerusalem now Earth bound.
A new Heaven and a new Earth,
have now both been given a new birth.
Oh, it is so dazzling to see
the heart overflows with ecstacy!
It's happening now as we live the prophecy,
of all that shall soon come to be.
The Light's descended
Mother Earth's ascended.
Some Earthlings, fallen panicking.
Beings of Light within them knowing
that the Time is here and it is now

that their Good Shepherd is here, somehow.
He comes to gather all His sheep
flooding them with waves of Love so deep.
An abundant shepherd, with lots to give, who
gathers them all — and that's me and you too.
Now in the safety of His pen,
they know the Love pure and peace like when
He had held them once so close
and their Life Force shone and rose,
as did their inward tranquility.
He always had had the ability
to make them like Him, shine,
to enliven their souls Divine!
In this New Heaven on Earth of His
there's no pain or suffering, only Bliss.

It's what we've all been waiting for,
Our pure state of being, before the fall.
Back to our pure state of perfection,
a brand-new start — OUR RESURRECTION!

Oh, Blessed Day

Dear God,
thank you for giving us warning signs and time before
the gates shut!
Before the Book of Love in half got cut
and saving all those souls, making Jesus' Life
worthwhile,
putting on His angelic face a smile
as He now leads His nation
generation after generation.
They come to Him adore,
in His full glorious heavenly lore.
They just want to be with Him,
pure and free inside, within.
In His Universe so pure,
They all rest, all secure.
They fervently worship at His feet
where God and Human Divinity meet.

Oh, Blessed Day you are come
to welcome the Heavenly Son
His New Kingdom of Life on Earth
peace, Love, harmony and mirth,
envelop them all, these Beings
beyond their wildest dreams!

Oh, Blessed Day you are come
as a new Dawn, dawns, a new Day's begun.
The radiance of the sun so bright
emitting Life and Love, giving Light,
making each and every ray,
in our beings there to stay.

Oh, Blessed Day you are come
long-awaited by everyone!
Hills, Mountains, Rivers and Falls,
all the Land that to you calls,
in expectant anticipation
to a broken Earth, bringing reparation.
A healing, a repair, a restoration
yearned for in eager expectation.

Oh, Blessed Day you are come
To welcome the Heavenly Son.
A new Dawn, dawns, a new Day's begun!
Long-awaited by everyone!

Leaping Legs, Skipping Feet

Skipping, dancing, leaping in the air
the New Jerusalem is now here.
Let's celebrate and have some fun,
The hosts of Heaven and us on Earth —
you, me, my Son and everyone.
We jump for joy, way up high
to the Heavens, the highest heights.
Twirling, singing, shrieks of laughter,
joy, love, peace forever after.
Just like a fairy-tale come true
This redemption for me and for you,
is now a Fait Accompli —
done — fully complete!

Through the door they've come,
your feet!
And whether weary
or blithely bouncy,
whether dreary
or somewhat flouncy,
Different feet, in various sizes,
have now come to claim their prizes.
As their feet have touched the ground
with a thump or a silent sound,

at the finish line marked out
across the Earth and throughout.

Jumping for exultation,
with no boundary or limitation
the feet bound in
through the door wherein,
lies the New Earth and Her King
in they gather, His praises sing.

God Speaks Through the Mist in Avalon

God speaks to me in the mist today
an important message to relay.
Shrouded in magic and mystery
a message seeped in this place's history,

On the side of the tor,
up upon the moor
veiled in a stillness and silence.
The message revealed
from the chaos concealed,
given to a lowly maid
as she stands praying in the shade.
Waiting for God to speak
to this maiden humble and meek.

"I come to you today
to say
that come what may
in the forthcoming days
amidst the mist and the haze
I shall be with you all —
My Will, Guide you all
My Peace, Strengthen you all
My Joy, Enliven you all

My Presence, Enlighten you all
My Love, Protect you all.

All of My Beloved ones who
Love Me like I love them too.
To them I shall come running,
as the New Earth comes into being.
Do not be afraid
just keep standing
unafraid, in the
sweet shade
of My Protection
which is a reflection
of My Power and Might.
It will protect quite a few
and, that Our dearest, includes you!

Yet, to some it will be a
Death Dark, slow
violent shaking as their bodies blow
out any light, want it removed
their actions not by Love approved.
Their lives dreary, dreadful and dark
their bodies weak, lacking spark.
Yet, to my Beloved ones who to Me come,
maybe many, maybe some,

My Heart will welcome into its core
where flowing, fresh waters of Life flow
Peace and rest they shall once more know.

Show them the way,
say to them as I say,
to come to the heart of God now.
Smell the roses in My Heart
exquisite perfume, all a part
and parcel of My Love for You
and all of those others who
rest in Me and I in them,
goodbye for now, until then!

Light Over Darkness Wins

God alone is our only fill
our souls' mission this to fulfil.
His Will be done in and through us all,
as we have finally heeded the call.
We come along in thousands, throngs,
gathering speed,
only of His Love having the need.
And that need is now fulfilled,
in each and every Soul and Spirit
abundant Love beyond all limit.
Music hums
to the beat of the drums
gathering the nations
without reservations
the influx of incoming pilgrims,
as Light over darkness wins!

The throngs gather by fresh waters flowing —
dazzling rivers all a-glowing,
shimmering silvery leaves
glowing gleaming sheaves
glittering sight
golden light
silvery bright

stepping sweet
Him to greet.
Arms outstretched,
He welcomes them back.
He then shuts the gate,
for at any rate
those not there, are now too late!

Those that are there and then,
know precisely when
He'll call out their name
they'll fully regain
their Life in Light
to everybody's sheer delight.
Oh! What a glorious day,
The New Heaven on Earth's here to stay!

The Virgin's Prayer
(For the Divine Earthly Mother)

The ministry of Love for which I have been ordained,
through the Love within me, as it's been sustained.
A delicate rose my being I gift to You,
with it I humbly ask, Your Holy Will to do.

As I am back home in Your House of Joy
back home where I belong, after so much toil,
grief, sadness, anguish, agony and pain —
Your Will be done — these never again
shall assail my being, almost destroying my Spirit.

The Law of God's Love, The Law Supreme
in every blade of grass, in every human being's
Heart, Mind, Body and Soul.
There in the trees, bees, birds, flowers, fish
The Law Divine a sumptuous Dish
of sustenance to the Human Spirit
of Love and Light Divine.

Keep my faith fruitful,
my love for You beautiful.
My light shining bright for all to see
to bring them back to You Son, so let it be.

As throngs of angels accompany me here,
wafting sweet heavenly music in my ear.
You descend once more upon the Earth
full of power, glory, love, life, light, a new Earth to give
birth.

In full glorious Heavenly regalia arrayed
Your Godhead ever-present, Your power sustained.
For You come in glory to claim Your own,
as they adore You on Your Heavenly throne.
Full of adoration and ardent devotion,
their hearts' love expands like a heavenly ocean
opening up wave after wave
with their love, themselves and all creation to save.
The Earthly Mother's Earth Divine
bringing back wholeness and making Her fine.
Allowing her, her beauty like the days of yore once
more —
to her renewed way of being, open the door.

Have Her Being healed and made whole,
may this be a part of our new sacred role.
To be there, proclaiming Her sacredness and power
which greed and lust do Her now devour.
Her beauty and sanctity must be adored
as her mutilated body is healed and restored.

May she not suffer and die due to greed
and may everybody acknowledge the need
for Her Sustenance abundantly and freely given
May Her body now depleted, be forever risen
resplendent with dazzling Life force abundant
a new way of being, the old way's redundant.

I Am Enough

'I AM' all that I need
It's all within me like a seed,
that needs watering and the light
not too dim, not too bright
to sprout and to flower
in full blossom, its true power.

The Father-Mother its soil,
as Angels diligently toil
to bring it all fully to life, so
to full bloom it will grow
and its full potential it will know.

Deep in the dark depths of the Earth below,
the seed slowly, begins to grow —
in the silence and the stillness
reaching up, into the light shoots out,
with rapturous joy it begins to sprout.

All its fragranced beauty celebrate, behold
glorious colour and scent renown'd,
an array of diamonds, rubies, sapphires, gold
the senses dance in its beauteous being
the naked eye's resplendent seeing.

You don't need faith as you do know
that as the seeds in the Earth doth grow,
and transform into bulbs exquisite —
you yourself like that gentle flower,
must go forth and claim your power.

Going Forth

Please, sweet, beloved Son give all the strength, courage
and words to your mum
everything she needs to go boldly ahead
to speak the Good News as You'd already said.
That we are the Beloved of God on High
Our place within Him, You do not lie.
His Essence within our being, making us One
Enlighten our minds
Open our hearts
Strengthen our bodies
Shine through our Beings
Ignite our Spark Divine.

We have awoken to the tricks of the dark side
How they lay their snares, their hands hide.
Making them the Masters of Illusion
As we all sleep in deceptive delusion
believing their insidious lies no more —
Deception is out through the door.

Now breaking free from the ties
of their devious deception
recognising it at its inception
acknowledging within the Truth,

Freedom, our own hearts soothe.

Our whole being is now set free
from lies, deceit, guilt and shame.
We are now able to be
pure, true and without blame.

The |Love of the Father, Mother and Son

The gentle sweetness of the Love of the Father-Mother
for each and every one of us, is like no other.
She-He worships the ground we walk on
and hence, to us She-He sends the Only Dearly Begotten
Son.

The heart of the Father-Mother calls
to break down barriers, to smash down walls
and to allow Her-His sweet Love reign therein,
to abide in your heart and dwell within.

Do not turn away in haste,
as all this Love will go to waste!
Well, it'll go to someone who relishes it
and wants to embrace it, every single bit.
It'll go to the ones who Her-Him adore
although at times they aren't so sure.
Yet, they keep the faith and the trust
that this Love and Light within them must
be allowed to shine and shimmer,
filled with hope, its gentle glimmer.
Their hearts awake,
so much at stake.
Death or Life?

Peace or Strife?
Awaken and know
that Her-His Love in you shall blossom and grow.
The Joy and Peace and Love already within
Will fill you up right to the brim!

The Whisper of Your Inner Voice

When there's nothing left on the outside,
everything's collapsed —
belief systems, families, houses, politics, countries,
churches, sects
there's absolutely nothing left!
Chaos, with nothing to hold onto,
to clutch at
to use as a staff
for support —
A moment of great power?
Or a moment to despair?
A moment to disintegrate?
Or a moment to repair?
A moment of sheer brokenness and vulnerability —
the time to take full responsibility.

Look inside
there's nowhere to hide.
There's nothing left,
except
you and your inner being
your Soul,
your Spirit,

your Truth.
Look, watch in the stillness of meditation,
allow the process of mediation
with Divine Love and Light now begin
in spite of the chaos, confusion and din.
Its quiet, almost inaudible voice
guides us amidst the carnage,
complete disintegration within and without.

A new being sprouts out
out of naught!
When naught is all there remains,
all's lost, no glittery earthly gains
nowhere to go, nowhere to hide,
only taking refuge in the Sound of Silence and Soul
inside.

It gets louder and clearer
the message it brings, coming nearer
Truth, Strength, Courage,
Love, Life, Light,
Compassion, Freedom
singing a song of joy and gladness
amidst the outer maddening madness
of complete and utter destruction.

And then in that desolate moment you hear your Inner
Voice speak:

"You are not weak,
as you've been told —
you are not a commodity to be sold,
you are not a cog in a machine,
you are not just here to shop and clean,
you are not stupid or a fool,
you are not here to be a corporate tool,
you are not here to serve the government,
you are not here to be the system's servant!

You are here, listen to me,
You are here, look and see
Open your eyes and ears
Eliminate all fears
Allow me to take the lead
and you shall become free, indeed!
Allow me to guide your way,
My Inner Law of Love to obey!
Allow me to instruct you in Truth and Authenticity
for that's the only way to be.
To live your Truth within you
is to love your God and Yourself too.

Have love and compassion for all others,
sisters, brothers, fathers, mothers
neighbours, co-workers, whoever they may be,
be kind and compassionate to all and you'll see
that the Truth guides you and sets you Free."

Your Truth
Your Life
Your Love
Your Compassion
Your Light
Your Joy
…emanating from within to the world,
sounding perhaps a bit absurd
is what will set you free,
to be the Being you were meant to be.

Free from the Dark that is now destroyed
a new life's created, the old's redeployed.
The greatest gift of God Divine and King
may His-Her musical symphony within ring
of the new found union within our hearts
putting back in place all the wounded parts
that have been shattered into a million pieces.
The heavenly kingdom in our Hearts restored

our soul within us is now renewed and adored.
Go within where God speaks to the Heart and bow
to the infinite, Eternal Truth, that you know.

The Red Admiral

It landed on the rocky, dry land
not on grass or any soft sand.
Originally, it fluttered its delicate wings,
as if my praises it silently sings.
A delicate Red Admiral in a deserted, dusty car park
A Lonely Lady, sad
the world situation being so bad.

Delighted at its sight
She stood still, as it might
suddenly flutter away and take flight.
Time stops.
She stands still.

The Red Admiral momentarily motionless,
addresses the Lonely Lady, listless.

"Fear not, Dearest beloved Mary,
for although always quite contrary
God has found favour in you
with His grace you, He'll imbue.
Do not be scared of any calamity
be relaxed, still full of serenity.
For the Lord God has promised His protection always

to those connected to His Being in Love Divine —
Nobody shall harm those who are mine!
Calamity shall strike, thunder may roar
Yet My beloveds to the Heavens shall soar.
Whilst still a human body inhabiting
My Love throughout it reverberating
Strength adorns its every pore,
Courage roars its mighty roar!
Your feet shall not be scorched or burnt
None of your mind, body and heart shall be hurt.
For I cloak you in My love Divine
within which all shall be fine.
I envelop you in love and peace
never-ending, unbound by a finite lease!
Infinite, Eternal, pure and unbiased -
A love freely given to all.
I urge all, to heed its call.
From the depths of my Being
within the all-seeing
ever-present love, pure light, and sacred sound
whence infinite joy and peace abound.
You were all created and lovingly made whole —
perfect. The enemy, then came and stole
energy pure and grace sublime,
You followed him, when you're actually mine!
I do not want you, to own,

I wish for you to enjoy the love that I have sown
and put into your being
always there, albeit not seen.
Gifted with the freedom to choose
at the high risk the connection to lose
your love, your fellowship and your friendship
and you losing your God-given creative craftsmanship.

Yet, as you have come back to me
With Me forever to be,
The whole of creation will follow suit
they'll realise it's the only route.
The path rocky, dry and full of dross,
Burdened by many a heavy cross.
Yet, each plant, tree, flower and bird
the sea, sun, sky, sand, all heard
the call of Love, they come to protect
as peace and joy within all they inject.
That peace and joy flowing from Me
Nature my physical expression, for you to see!

Through the touch of the gentle breeze
you rest in courage, full of ease.
Through the chirping of the bird
you hear all the messages that must be heard.
Through the smiling flowers bright

you perceive all beauty and delight.
Through the sky so blue and eternal
a pure reflection of your Being's internal
and external Infinity
beyond boundaries — one Unity.
Drop the labels and the names
abadon guilt and all the shames.
Carry yourself tall and upright,
Claiming your power with all your might.
Do not let anyone say you cannot, no —
Your reclaimed power them now show!
Not an arrogance, or a pride
not ego-cherishing, rude or snide.
A strength in and of love, Supreme
from Source, within your own Being, beam
with peace, forgiveness and abounding joy.
A sea of swarming buzzing bees
Come on, Humanity, get off your knees!

Rediscover that Love which binds us all
Listen carefully to its silent call.
Allow your heart to be touched by its gentle caress
as its mark on your heart it yearns to impress.
There is no other way to be
Only in ME, in Infinity.
There is no other way to rock —

heed my call, your heart unblock.
This is the only path to Life,
free from suffering, free from strife.
When all live through love, not fear
When all the call of love do hear
When all re-open and re-connect
without Fear, this will inject
Freedom back into slave-bound minds
Light into each being's space finds
Love into harassed hearts replenished
Health into bodies restored.
All shall be made whole once more.
Renewed, returned back to the Core
from whence All came and shall return,
each their heavenly place shall earn.

And to those who choose not
their bodies shall rot
in slime and sludge.
They shall not budge
from the tyranny
of my enemy.

The invitation is open to all,
heed the call, heed the call!
Return to your Source, at your core,

of all creation, of Universes, of ALL.
Come back home to Love, heed its call, heed its call!
Return back to the Heart of God, once more —
Now and forevermore!